the unbearable beauty

*poems & practices
for being alive*

annabelle blythe

THOUGHT
CATALOG
Books

THOUGHTCATALOG.COM

THOUGHT CATALOG Books

Copyright © 2023 Annabelle Blythe.

All rights reserved. No part of this book may be reproduced or transmitted in any form or any means, electronic or mechanical, without prior written consent and permission from Thought Catalog.

Published by Thought Catalog Books, an imprint of Thought Catalog, a digital magazine owned and operated by The Thought & Expression Co. Inc., an independent media organization founded in 2010 and based in the United States of America. For stocking inquiries, contact stockists@shopcatalog.com.

Produced by Chris Lavergne and Noelle Beams
Art direction and design by KJ Parish
Creative editorial direction by Brianna Wiest
Circulation management by Isidoros Karamitopoulos

thoughtcatalog.com | shopcatalog.com

First Edition, Limited Edition Pressing
Printed in the United States of America.

ISBN 978-1-949759-72-3

the unbearable..................................9
the beautiful....................................65

for the parts you've kept hidden

like you, i have been through the unbearable—i have lost myself more times than i can count. like you, i have felt wildly alone, directionless, unsafe, and deeply unknown. like you, i have met many moments in which i wondered if i could keep going. but i have seen how beautiful this life is when we pay attention. i have found the beauty that lives within the dark. i offer these words as a bridge through the invisible. a tapestry of the intangible threads of life. a reminder of what remains in both the unbearable and in the beautiful. allow these poems and practices to be soothing balms. use them as tools. use them as tonics. use them for your actualization, your discernment, your deconditioning, your becoming. take them literally, figuratively, or something else. let them in like a friend, a teacher, an enemy to your self abandoning. imagine with them, experiment with them, become with them. on the other side i hope you find something new, or discover something lost.

i'll meet you there.

the unbearable

i think it all started
when i left the womb
when i went from being in a body
to being a body
with nothing around me but air
suddenly incomplete

the unbearable beauty

everything we fear can be tied back to our fear of death
but i say i'm not afraid
so it's myself i run from
in the mirror instead

sometimes i feel like all i've ever done is echo somebody else
i wish someone could tell me how to be myself

the unbearable beauty

my first breath was not my own
it took three months for my body to learn
i grew up breathing into closed rooms
unable to find the air
i grew up reaching out
begging for contact
finding nothing but space
i was marked by a deep hunger
i felt a wildness inside of me
that i could not put into words
i was told i was out of control
i feared i could not control myself
i disciplined myself into an act of disappearance
i am still trying to come out of hiding
i am still trying to tilt my face up to the sky
and trust
that everything in me is allowed to be here

how to ruin your life:

do something that only someone else wants
try to put your heart in a box
hold on to your obsessions

the unbearable beauty

things to waste your energy on:

someone else's idea of beauty
a costume for someone you wish you were
someone else's dream

everything in the room was that honey yellow
that late september golden hour
and we were in brooklyn
and it wasn't the first time my imagination
ran wild for someone
in a room where the paint was peeling
my vision blurred looking at you
but when i focus in on my memory
i see it now

the sunflowers were rotting in the corner
but i wanted to pretend
even if only for the few hours
before the room went dark

the last time i broke my own heart

the unbearable beauty

*sometimes we must give in to our obsessions
to remember how they burn*

i thought we would be good together
but the flowers were rotting in the corner

this was not a place where the living
and the beautiful
could survive

pay attention to who and what you reach for

when you're not fully alive in your life

pay attention to what reaches back

ways i have let my life force escape:

i ignored my hunger
i called it love
i ignored that i wanted her
i ignored that i needed my ancestors
i pretended that it was okay to wake up
every day exhausted by what i should do
i tried to contort myself into the shape of
someone who had something i didn't
i stayed after my heart told me to go
i asked for milk where only water was being offered

when i have felt not enough i have been
holding a part of myself back.
when i have felt too much i have been in the
presence of people who cannot hold all of me.

these can be interchanged.

i learned the rules of leaving my body in the womb of a woman who could not learn how to be in hers. i learned the rules of leaving my body when i was birthed into a being that could not be breathed. i learned the rules of leaving my body the first time i opened my mouth and nothing was there to fill it. i learned the rules of leaving my body the first time my body asked for more. i learned the rules of leaving my body the first time that i was told that i was too much, that i was a bordered thing playing outside of its limits. i learned the rules of leaving my body the first time i was told bodies are not good. i learned the rules of leaving my body the first time hands went where they were not allowed. i learned the rules of leaving my body the first time i was told bodies are not god. i learned the rules of leaving my body the first time i watched someone walk away as their voice was in my head telling me that they would stay. i learned the rules of leaving my body when i discovered that my body was built to hold pain. i learned the rules of leaving my body when i learned that truth lives in the body but i could live out a lie.

a practice for comparison

stay sensitive to beauty
when our eyes find their way so strongly to one thing, we must do everything we can to look in a different direction. soften your gaze. soften the stories that tell you this world speaks of beauty in a way that makes room only for one. be willing to let your eyes wander. notice how there is beauty to be found even in the most unexpected places. how there is beauty in what is often overlooked. if you can't see it—look a little closer. now believe me when i say that you can live as if there is more than one story worth telling.

let the competition end
see that it is not the thing they have that you want—it is how they are connected to their essence. use this as an invitation to connect to yours. you contain the energy of lifetimes inside of you. all you must do is notice when your whole body is paying attention.

we are taught to fear the ones
with revolution in their eyes
and call them
the other

you can take someone to the most sacred place and they can still not be able to see it. i have learned that we are like this when we look at each other.

questions to ask at the end:

what have you had to give up to be fully alive?

when have you had to break your
heart in order to listen?

where have you found yourself again?

when will you decide to give us a full telling?

the unbearable beauty

you cannot reject the shadow and expect to embody the light

i am wondering about original thought
if i have ever had one in my life
or if i am just a collection of colliding atoms
stolen from foreign places
i thought were home

the unbearable beauty

our skin tells stories of who we are
and who we have been
the horror
the relief
that nothing is ever truly hidden

we look for answers where we will not find them. in the ones that made us up from cells and magic. in the body we crawled our way out of, unable to breathe. we look for understanding in the place we most expect to find it. wanting to dig our way back into the womb. the walls too fragile to contain us. so we dig into the red dirt of the desert. seeking wholeness in the nectar of the earth. in the circling of smoke. in the shadow of the moon like an invitation. we look in the ways our bodies move like animals as we navigate the dark. we look with the hands of a child, open, waiting. we look as saints. as sinners. we stretch our necks and look further. to symbols, to celestial bodies, to the invisible. as if only we could reach through the sky to beyond and climb our way out of the question.

the unbearable beauty

we get lost
somewhere between dreaming
and the unimaginable dark

don't hide from the life within you

a practice for when you no longer know who you are

eye gaze with yourself in the mirror
sit in front of a mirror. look into your own eyes. come back to your body. keep looking. notice who and what you find. notice how this goes beyond what you look like, what the outside world thinks of you. see if you can sense your spirit. see if you can sense that love is what looks back.

become someone new
maybe it's okay. maybe you don't need to go back to who you were. maybe you can become someone new. maybe there's more than one you to find. maybe you are bigger than something that can be defined. maybe the possibilities of your life are extending outward like a branch. maybe the path you take doesn't matter as much as you think. maybe there is no better or worse. maybe you will always end up in the same place. maybe the only thing to do is to follow your inner voice above all else. maybe all you have to do in this life is remember what your voice sounds like when it speaks.

life is short, but existence is long.
you will get to it when you are ready.

do what you need to do to get whole

i wanted something real but i didn't know how to ask for it. my tongue couldn't find the right shape to ask for what i needed. like the ask was too heavy. like the ask was begging to crawl into a space it wasn't welcome. like the ask was reaching into an empty cave, expecting to feel something alive. like something in my body didn't want me to find my way back to her. i wanted to find the place where i separated young from old and let the little one inside of me sit alone in the dark. i wanted to find where truth lives in my skin. i wanted to go back to where i let go of her hand. i wanted to try again. i wanted her to stand on top of everything she asked for and cry out into ears that could listen. i wanted to soothe her when she was afraid of being left *(and everyone always left)*. i wanted to let my eyes open. i wanted to see her. i could only make out her shape, moving and bending the way that light does. i wanted her to know that i'm learning, now, how not to leave her. i wanted to let my heart open as my eyes do. i wanted to keep her safe. i felt her in my spine. i wanted to make her real. i wanted to let her in. i wanted to let her out. i opened my mouth.

the unbearable beauty

maybe to love someone is only to dare to see them fully
maybe to love yourself is the same

my least favorite part of living is when it feels like an act. for most of my life, being in my body has felt like a performance. a performance of survival. of desire. of goodness. sometimes i can't even tell that i'm performing until long after it's done and i'm lying alone in the dark. sometimes i can't hold a conversation because i can see that they are performing, too. it's taken me thirty years to understand what it means to be in my body. most of that time i spent trying to figure out what it meant to be in someone else's. i did this so that i could figure out how to act. i learned my lines well. i forgot that i was performing. i existed in a kind of haze. i feel like i didn't know a real person until i was seventeen. a substitute teacher, unclear how he got the gig. he sat by our table of misfits and told us that we didn't have to do what we were told. that if we had other dreams and ideas, to trust them. this energy stayed with me as i walked out of the classroom and stayed with me on the subway home and stayed with me all the way until i walked in the front door of my father's house and opened my mouth. the intermission was over. in the years that followed i left my body more and more and wondered why i wasn't brave enough to go beyond the stage. and then i met death and the whole theater lit up and i realized no one was watching. that i was surrounded by an infinity mirror of stages but there was no one to listen. that we were all echoing back the same act to each other. that so few people existed outside those dark rooms. i looked for the door. i walked down the aisle not knowing. i'm still trying not to look back.

the unbearable beauty

who are you when the performance is over?
where are you when no one else is around?

you can stand in front of someone
and offer them everything
or you can jump into a dark lake
and ask it to take everything that's dark within you

the unbearable beauty

i see the masks you are wearing
and still
i want you to be the first to reveal
my mind plays tricks on me
the kind that were never mine to learn
i want you to see that your mind plays tricks on you too
i want you to question who taught you
i want you to look out at what we call terrible
and see how we still find our way back to the living
i want you to hear me
but the words won't leave my throat
i want you to see me
but i have spent too long in the quiet

my vices have knives
i ask what they can teach me
i pray they won't cut me open
(*i pray that they will*)

life has a tendency to go like this: when we need to leave someone, somewhere, some way of being that is comfortable for the wrong reasons—we are given a kick. the power goes out for weeks. a room sets on fire. we lose an object that was held too tightly. our bodies begin to speak in metaphors. ignoring the early warning signs turns the alarm bells into sirens. we can end up in crisis. in hospital beds. in situations that demand us back into our body after so long living outside of it. how do we know when it's over? we don't, because knowing is of the mind. knowing is logic and reason, and sometimes these things never come. we don't because our bodies will tell us. despite all we have been taught to fear, our intuition is a guidance system. this neutral, in-the-moment knowing speaks in a different language than the fearful loops of anxious thought. we have been conditioned to dissociate. to view our bodies as machines rather than divine guidance systems and wise teachers, to prize our minds over our instinctual senses. forgive yourself—it's near impossible to feel enough to listen to the first whispers when they are perpetually starved. but we must begin to listen. we must not deny ourselves this practice just because we cannot get there through a quick fix. there is no ten-step guide or thirty-day regime that will bring you back to your own nature. what is required is a gentleness that can be strengthened over a lifetime. we must practice the simplest things like slowing down, resting more. we must practice connection, sensitization, and filtering what we are told through our own awareness. this is not a skillset. this is a life practice. this is how we will know when it's over. this is how we stay alive.

blythe

listen closely to what your life is telling you

the unbearable beauty

when you are 17 and think your life is over
when you are 22 and acting like somebody's mother
when you are 31 and finding your way back to youth
when you are 55 and crawling your way out of a womb
keep going

aliveness is calling
like sunlight
it is a warmth that is hard to look directly into
but all beautiful things ask us first to burn
all beautiful things will eventually be set free

it has been said that falling in love happens like this—slowly, and then all at once. but this happens with places, too. with the inevitable unravellings of the versions of ourselves. we say til death do us part but do not stop to ask what death we are referring to. we say forever without looking towards the horizon of the version of ourselves we claim to be in this moment. i think we lose the things we hold so dearly in order to find the shape of our own being no longer wrapped around something that wasn't us to begin with. i think life is the endless pursuit of falling apart because what we are left with at the end of it all is that which could never be threatened from the start. i look into you and i look into a million versions of what could be, of all there ever was. i am learning that beginnings are endings, too.

i'm looking for a practice to stay alive
i'm looking for a practice to feel real
i'm looking for a practice to survive
i'm looking for a practice to not be so scared of loving
i'm looking for a practice to burn it all to the ground
i'm looking for a practice to stop performing
i'm looking for a practice to build a bridge
i'm looking for a practice to stop feeling so alone
i'm looking for a practice to remember what is real
i'm looking for a practice to no longer feel threatened
i'm looking for a practice to feel like being here is enough
i'm looking for a practice

he told my eyes looked like honey
he told me sadness made them thick
i said that wasn't his to find

he asked me if i was okay
i told him that okay wasn't something i intended to find
that you can spend a lifetime doing
everything in your power to be okay
or you can join the fullness of being alive

a practice for self-love

notice the beauty in a broken object
notice how the light reflects on broken glass like a million suns staring back at you. notice how the exit wounds of your old identities invite you into a healing. notice how we rise from the ashes of our creations. notice how your body continues, without your trying.

remember that your life is here
don't miss the living minutes of your life waiting for a static moment. don't lose yourself in wishing for the future. be wary of a world that asks you to be somewhere else.

sometimes it's good to be somewhere
you wouldn't have chosen
for a while
to take ten steps back
to see how you've changed
by what you've seen and where you've been
how you are entirely new
we can't experience the same thing twice
we can't be the same version of ourselves forever
to love yourself
to love someone else
is to want to reread their heart again and again
each time an experience of something entirely new
give yourself this gift
as you walk through the geographies
of who and where you've been

i have been spiraling
spiraling
spiraling
you see me in the same place
to you i am within the same shape
i wish you could go as far as i have
i wish you could travel higher with me

how to care for a mind that tries to destroy you:

wear clothes that allow you to be present in
your body without criticizing the size of it

drink more water, for the way it clears you

bathe with salt, for the way it cleans you

cut your hair, for the way it removes
what has grown stale

speak kind words to the parts of
you that got left behind

gaze softly at who you've become

the most precious thing you can learn in this life:

when to protect your energy
when to reveal
how to know the difference

the unbearable beauty

it was night but all the flowers were alive
they reflected a surreal light
i think it was you
showing me what it was like to be with the living

a practice for when you feel alone in this world

notice how the world is constantly showing you mirrors of yourself
in the way you catch your reflection in a car window. in the way you find heart-shaped rocks when you need to be reminded that love is real. in the way you lose magic and then find dappled sunlight showering on you like a prayer. in the way that just when you can't take the gray anymore, the sky breaks open on a tuesday afternoon.

notice how even what seems surreal and out of place is
still beautiful
find beauty in the lost objects. in the trees growing out of the sidewalks. in the flowers that have grown over the stop sign. in the chair found in the middle of the forest. in the shock of a purple flower in the desert. in the unexpected discovery on the walk you take day in and out. in the oldest face in the room. in the clouds in june.

a practice for self-sabotage

pick up yesterday's clothes from the chair
allow your ideas of what is true to dissolve with yesterday's stories, worries, and ghosts. although you may cling too tightly, the constructs you attach yourself to are not actually you. the ways you identify who you are in this world likely aren't either. the loops in your mind that you think are you can be dissolved in any moment by connecting with the parts of you that stay steady underneath it all. you never have to carry who you were yesterday into today. every day, each moment has the opportunity to be completely fresh. cleanse your space. cleanse your body. remove a little bit of clutter. move to calm your mind. write it all down. notice how each inhale creates space in your body. notice what that does to your mind. do what you need to do to feel clear even if only for a moment.

be honest with the truth trying to get out
truth is inescapable. what you see as sabotage is often an act of getting out of the wrong life. there is a truth underneath it all, trying to get out. even if it's crawling, kicking, screaming, hurting along the way. consider that maybe your resistance is just saying *not this* or *not yet*. be open to this being a neutral discovery. looking back you may feel you have lost something beautiful. maybe you feel this has happened more than once. but i invite you to see that it was often only a possibility, or an image of beauty that you were not able to feel beautiful in. maybe you needed more time, maybe you needed to heal, maybe you needed to learn more, surrender more. maybe your nervous system wasn't ready. maybe they weren't the one. maybe it was never supposed to be that way, you had

to continue, you had to leave, you had to grow into yourself, you had to let something fall away. what we judge is what we create suffering from. it's easy to look back and think of who or what we could become. it's more courageous to accept all that is and look to who we are becoming. now, this does not mean that it has to feel fair. that there are no great tragedies. that you will never experience loss. you will. your heart is here to be broken. this is a part of being alive. you can fight this unbearable truth or you can see it for its beauty. you can become curious about fully being here more than trying to cut off a necessary part of the experience of the living. you can discover that everything is a portal if you let it be.

a practice for when you can no longer
find the ground beneath you

welcome in the parts of you that are scared
this is not the time to deny reality. this is not the time to push through. this is the time to allow dissolution, while you acknowledge the parts of you that want to hold on. this is the time to forgive yourself, over and over. this is the time to speak kindly to your inner child. the part of you that is most scared. this is the time to hold your own hand. to not cast blame. to accept what is so that you can remember what stays true.

remember that you have always continued
despite it all, you have always found your way back through. if you are reading this, you are still breathing. if you are reading this, you are strong enough to hold fluctuations. the small dips. you are steadier than that. you can trust yourself more than that. trust in your strength. if not yours, all of the ones who have come before you. all of your ancestors known and unknown walking at your back. all of your guides moving invisibly in front. all versions of self past and future hold steady at your side. you are not alone. remember that even when you have lost everything you believed to make you who you are, you remained. trust in what remains.

how to be human

remember that you can make no promises
finding certainty is a lifelong chase. finding an identity may be just as elusive. we can devote ourselves to our own souls. we can find a calling. we can find each other. we can lose it all. none of this is a mistake. in this life, no future can be promised. and yet here you are, with a part of you that knows nothing that is real can be lost.

remember that you can break the ones you tried to make
break the promise you made to let parts of yourself hide. begin to allow every part of you to exist. allow your contradictions. to the parts of your life that you are growing too big for--let go of the promise to stay. you need room to become all that you are here to be. be brave with your life. your anger is an invitation into your own becoming. your grief is begging you to tell the full story. be brave enough to ask for something bigger. when you are asked to begin again, believe that there is life beyond the one you dreamed of while living in your old one.

the unbearable beauty

i became whole because
a woman entered my life

it took me years to recognize her face in the mirror

a practice for releasing attachment

relax your hands
notice the shapes your hands make. notice what you hold onto, long after it has left. relax your grip. you have been carrying all of this for a long time. release what feels heavy. there is nothing in this life that needs you to cling to it in order for it to thrive, not even life itself. what we hold tightly is often what slips through our fingers in the most violent of ways. you can welcome in the world with an open palm. you can meet the ones you love from this place of receptivity. you can find what it is you truly want to hold.

remember impermanence
there is nothing in this human life that will stand the test of time, not even life itself. being present with what is is not asking you to deny death. meeting death while you are alive is not asking you to surrender being alive. find beauty in the fact that existence has carried on long before you, and will continue long after. it is impossible to feel this in every moment, but see if you can find a pause in a quiet morning to remember. the impermanence of everything is what makes it all worth living. let yourself exist in both.

stop fearing love

you are human, as much as you may not want to be. if you are reading this now—you are here, in a body, on an earth that contains more beauty and pain than one person could ever hold alone. we attach, we face loss, we begin again. this is how we are. there is something in seeking non-attachment that goes against our very nature. it is our nature to connect in a way that is warm. there is something too gentle in us to be unattached without going cold. with nothing or no one to attach to as a child, you wouldn't be here. human relationships require expectations. human love requires attachment. we cannot survive for long alone. attachment is a sliver within the body of desire, the wanting of something bigger. with no desire to expand your experience, you wouldn't be here. with no attachment, our imaginations would remain in the clouds. the very beauty of this human experience has a piece of holding on within it. it is okay to hold from love. it is okay to know when to let go. this discernment is paramount, and will take you breaking your own heart to learn. do not run from this. this is why we are here.

a practice for dissolving the ego

climb onto the kitchen counter
connect to your inner child. do the opposite of what you were told. find new perspectives. look at something differently. look at the ocean upside down. when you are walking in a city, look up. when a child points, pay attention.

ask about love in a different language
go where you don't speak the language. go where you feel scared but your spirit is calling. be humbled by not being able to translate your internal experience as freely. open your heart. notice what eludes language. risk it all for that.

remember that you're only human
remember that you're not special. remember that everyone is. remember that to think you could dissolve an aspect of this human experience while in it is the real absurdity. stop thinking you would be more worthy without an ego. stop thinking you already are. stop missing the point. stop trying to get out alive. forgive yourself for trying.

the beautiful

*i asked where to find what is holy and
was told to turn towards myself*

on the third day
i was terrified
and all i wanted to do was cut this life in half
to crawl back
to ignore the clear part of me beaming brightly up ahead
telling me that i won't get everything that i want
threatening me that i'll get something more

these days i reach for her hand

i know how to become someone else in a calendar year more than i know how to stay the same.

everything else feels like pretend.

for the longest time
i believed that the part of me that was the strongest
was the one calling into an empty house
asking for
belonging

and after all of this
it turns out
of all of my parts
the one wanting to be
free
would win
every time

everything the secret part of you has dreamed is true

the unbearable beauty

i no longer want to leave no trace
my ghost will be known
i will go to war to be known by love
i am trying to show myself to you
while everything in me wants to hide
the parts of me that rub lip stains off of paper cups
and dig my trash to the bottom of the bin
i will pour your water first
and ask for forgiveness
before we have even met
i will apologize
i will trust that you know me better
even as you view me through a distorted lens
my goodness like a funhouse mirror
i want to be known for the parts with clear edges
even as my identity blurs
for the first time
i want to be alive more than i do not
and some days
this feels like a promise i fight to keep
i want to fight to be known
i want to see more people that are real
i want to be one of them

blythe

all of the dreams i didn't know i had have come true

the unbearable beauty

a girl let go of her ego
so a woman could open
to the way things are

a prayer
written to be read out loud, into the mirror

i am a mountain. i create my own gravity, and i have the entirety of the earth beneath my feet. there is no amount of weight i cannot hold. the walls around me may shake, but i am unmovable. i am my own teacher of steadiness as i hold my own center. connected to my center, i have a presence that holds eyes across a vast distance. i am a mountain. there are no limits to the spaces i can hold myself in and breathe myself into. all of the different parts of me make up the constellations i am growing into. all of the different parts of me are welcome in this unshakable home. i am of the earth and going back into her. the doors were never locked, and i am here, always waiting, at home in my own sky.

the unbearable beauty

*i close my eyes and imagine all of the
versions of myself i have not met yet*

when i was nineteen, my friend died on the day we were supposed to meet after a long summer. his life was taken outside of the restaurant where we first shared the stories of ourselves with each other. i did not have a full understanding of time before then. time felt like a boundless thing. an outstretched hand, inviting me in, never making direct contact. and there it was, hitting my body in the grief—it was all going to end. just like the young life on the cobblestone streets. a version of myself died the day i found out, and i began again. i began to live as if i was being chased. i became hungry for timeless things. my body and brain were drunk on urgency looking for some kind of salvation. i prayed and i preyed for more time in between bed sheets, in clouds of smoke, dressed in all white at the ends of the earth. i tried to find more waking minutes all the while missing the point entirely—that my life was not a checklist of people and places and possibilities to run through as quickly as my body would let me. that life was not chasing me through its winding streets. that my vision blurs when i run so quickly. it took me years to realize that i could find a lifetime of tenderness in the smallest of moments if my whole body was paying attention. like in the way our fingertips met in the dark, even if only once.

i understand, now, that it is not the amount of time we have been given, but how fully we can be here that matters most.

i didn't know who i was until i knew someone who wasn't anymore. we don't know who we are until we touch the edges of feeling. until we stumble into loss and its sacred cracks. until we are pushed into grief and its sacred portals. the way we choose to continue in the wake of what we knew. the way some of us cannot bear it. *i forgive you. i forgive you*. this life is full of so many things human hands were not shaped to hold. i only know how to keep going through my belief in what exists beyond the borders of our skin. *i love you for trying.* please, let's spend a few of our living minutes together. we never know when we will be out of time.

blythe

it will be beautiful, even if it is brief

a practice for loss

understand what you lose
our hands can hold nothing in this life. not truly. our own bodies will be given back to the earth. to say that we are our bodies is to miss something essential; to say we are not our bodies is to miss the point. i have spent time with masters who have one foot in another world—their body is still here, but something else has gone entirely. i have watched beings drift away entirely.

and what you never will
no matter what you believe, notice what lives on. the memory, the feeling, the way i can imagine you sitting next to me here and feel your head resting on mine. the way this makes me know that i am never alone. see them in the light, in the way that you are becoming something entirely new in their wake. believe me when i say i didn't know who i was until i knew someone who wasn't anymore. and all i had left were scars from their laughter that cut the room in half. and all i had left was the memory of their body next to mine. and all i had left was the replay of sitting on the edge of a volcano in the dark. and all i had left was the purple of tuesday turning into wednesday. and all i had left was the cold air scratching at my lungs. and all i had left were the clear skies of scotland. and all i had left was everything i still believed to be true.

believe them to be true

a practice for suffering

lay it all on the ground
your body. your mattress. your ideas. the manuscript. the photographs. the relics. lay it as close to the earth as your mind will let you. bury it in the ground if you can. keep it close to the ground to see it for what it is, taken off of its higher place. remember how we will all end up in the same place.

pay attention
it is often not until something is lost that we feel its presence. this is a portal to pay attention. to reimagine how it is that we are living. to end. to begin. to notice what your life is telling you. the good stuff is quiet, but the god stuff is quieter. listen closely.

reasons to do, to end, or to continue

1. you are becoming something new
2. you are living more simply
3. your body is speaking in metaphors
4. your life is sending smoke signals
5. you have returned to the living after a while away
6. an old part of you is begging for a funeral
7. your body feels liberated
8. you feel soothed when you're in it
9. your heart is opening
10. your inner child has sharper edges in your mind's eye
11. you no longer miss the point

you keep going for love. for the small moments that make all of the unbearable worth living. you keep going for the beauty. for the hope that because your human eyes have seen pure magic before it can happen again. you keep going because the third day doesn't last forever. you keep going because it is an honor to be on this earth. you keep going because you decide to give it all up to something bigger. you keep going because you want to find what is good. you keep going because you want to find what is god. you keep going because you love the smell of her neck and the way you feel when you place your hands on your own heart and say *i'm here*.

the unbearable beauty

maybe you're stuck
or maybe you're spiraling
just farther along the same path

how to change your life

change your socks at noon
we find the imprints we made yesterday again and again. we pick a favorite street, a favorite chair. we hold our bodies in the same way when we lean on the kitchen counter in the dark. our lips curl around familiar and unfamiliar glasses in a familiar pattern. we find hydration. we live our lives like the next is expected and feel disheartened when nothing shifts. we take the same shapes and are disappointed at the appearance of our shadow. a conscious altering is a call back to the spontaneity that is within the nature of being alive. an inspired left instead of a habitual right. a seemingly insignificant choice made at noon. a way to create something entirely new. this life works in ripples, and you never know what you will change.

do what you need to do to get whole
we will do anything to get out of our bodies. we will spend lifetimes trying to figure out what it means to be in a body that is not ours. we will give it all up for lust. we will pour all of our energy into everything but the art of living. we will go home every night to full homes and yet feel an emptiness in the space that is our true home within. we will live spiritually

starved, wondering why there is an insatiable hunger inside of us that we cannot name. we will run out of ourselves, again and again, abandoning the things we were told not to carry any longer. we will play by their rules and hold on until we drown. if we are lucky, we will experience a moment when we land back in our bodies like something shot out of a cannon in reverse. if we are ready, we will take this as a marching order. if we are brave, we will find our way across the foreign landscapes that exist inside of us. if we are wise, we will set the ghosts free. when it is time, we will find our way back home.

be willing to give it all up
we cling to what's ours. we cling to who we've been. we want what we've been told we should have. we run up against time, ourselves, and each other. we think *it shouldn't be like this*. we think *there should be more than this*. when in reality, all you have to do is try not to break under the unbearable, or lose yourself completely in the beauty. give it all up because none of what you cling to is yours. give it all up knowing that what is real will remain. that this life will ask you to give everything, but in return will give you even more.

blythe

we become what we long for or what we most fear

stop trying to become the shape of
something that is not you
let go of the love that grew away from you
leave the rooms that could not hold you
stop listening to the voices that try to silence you
listen closely to what your life is telling you
there was never anything wrong with you

a practice for making the right choice

go to a body of water and ask for your mind to be cleared

remember that choices are portals, not endings

make the good choice. make the wrong choice. make the good bad right wrong choice. chase after the right things. chase after the wrong things. make a lot of money. lose a lot of money. find a passion. give it all up. become good at something. get bored of it. crack your heart open a sliver. be open to that sliver becoming a portal. move countries. and again. try to learn a new language. fail. kiss the wrong person. break your own heart. get stitches. have your heart broken. scream until your lungs burn. wonder if you've ever had an original thought. call your mother. sit in rooms where you are the youngest. sit in rooms where you are the oldest. make friends with people who know more than you. accept that you know nothing. play pretend. play authenticity. tell the truth. remember that you have no idea who you are. ask why you're here. disappear for a month. ruin your life. let go. come back. go in. try again. let your ego die. keep going.

there are moments in this life that you cannot move away from. i have found myself calling this a *forced surrender.* i have found myself here more than once. i have found that this kind of surrender occurs in two parts. the abandonment of who and what i have been, without yet knowing what i am being asked to become. like how salt dissolves into water at the right capacity—life will often ask this much. this is rarely something i ask for. this is always something i need. this is the dissolution. *this is part one.* in this place of pure potential, i have watched myself want to become tight. i have seen my natural urge to close up like a flower bud that isn't ready. like a living thing that doesn't trust the sun. when i go into this place of guarding myself from the world, the process of dissolution that this surrender requires leaves me feeling lost. it is like my insides have spilled all over the floor and no one has given me any direction on how to put myself back together again. it is like i no longer know what it means to be myself. allowing is what happens when you have the courage to stay fallen apart. it is the choice to stay open. it is the choice to look at that which was once hidden inside of you, now out in the open, and to notice what calm space has been left in its wake. it is the choice to pay attention to what life starts to slow-drip into you to fill the space this surrender has created. *this is part two.* if you dare to live this life in a way that is asking to fully be here—life will ask you this much in return. to dissolve, forgiving yourself for not being what you want. to allow, finding the beauty in who it is you might become.

you are not here to perform your best performance
you are here to dissolve and allow
dissolve and allow
dissolve and allow
dissolve
allow
dissolve
allow
dissolve
allow
dissolve

a practice for humility

lose everything you love
you are alive. you are here. this is the way it is.

over and over
as long as you continue to live. your heart will continue to be broken. this is not because you are here to suffer. this is because you are here to open.

get still enough to see what is left
loss is a portal. the breaking is an opening. let the space fill your eyes. let your heart become something new. notice what is there. take refuge in what remains. give your life to this. let this be your ground.

the unbearable beauty

your life will bloom when you stop
going to war with your nature

blythe

how to get whole:

draw a circle—this is your life
put yourself in the center of it

stay until you hit the edges

a practice to create safety

feel your feet
remember that all you have is this moment. remember that you have been okay in every moment leading up to this, even when you felt far from it. remember that you are held here. feel gravity. feel your feet. feel your power. feel what connects you to this earth and what connects this earth back to you. look up.

go out on your own
move away from what you have known. move towards what you have dreamed. trust that it is safe for you to do this. stop trying to inhabit someone else's life. start honoring the one that lives within you. stop telling yourself you need all the answers. be gentle with yourself. try not to hide.

you have existed
long before this earth
and you will remain
long after
the final burst of light
goes out

you were born from darkness
merging with light
and miracles
like you
cannot be
destroyed

a practice to feel real

go to a third space
we must exist beyond the suspension between work and home. we must not lose sight of each other. when we live our lives too long in a place of disconnection, the world goes dark. we forget that there are others like us, too. no matter how much you love to be alone—go somewhere else. a library. a cafe. if you are lucky, a park. a space distinct from work and home. a space where you can witness other humans, being. our bodies are magic, and for many of us, just sitting in a space with others allows our nervous systems to regulate and our minds to slow. there is space for your body to take over. stay a while.

drink something hot
let the warmth be an invitation, a ritual, a welcoming. allow yourself to care for yourself. allow yourself to take your time.

let the performance end

human rituals that make me feel real:

buying a lamp to call a place home
lingering in doorways to say i belong
bathing in salt, in all of its forms
letting my body rest for no reason
movie theaters, and the feeling of leaving one into the dark
noticing dappled sunlight, and how it shifts
hands, and their language
kissing in another language
writing on paper
leaving a note behind
leaving nothing behind
the way my eyes find the horizon
the way my eyes found you, every time
falling in love
not being afraid

how to be free

lay on the ground
the biggest secret of your life is that you do not have to do or be anything other than here in order to hold value. you are not here to earn. you are not here to owe. it is safe for you to rest. if your body is exhausted, lay it down. if it feels urgent, lay it down. if everything feels like a threat, lay it down. if everything feels like an ending, lay it down. if you've lost all sense of center, lay it down. if your mind is so loud that you can no longer listen, lay it down. the urgency isn't real, or yours. right here, right now—you are the answer to everything you have ever asked. you are more than enough.

remember your divinity
your soul is so much bigger than your human to-do lists. your soul is the invisible force that asks you to continue. your soul is the piece that breathes even in the most unbearable circumstance. no one ever said it would all be fair. no one ever said your heart wouldn't break. no one ever said there wouldn't be a million injustices to rage against. but trust me when i say—your soul is free.

blythe

we walk into the invisible
into the great unknown
hoping to find each other
and you say there is no beauty to be found

the unbearable beauty

your light hits on everything
wait for the ones who can see it

(look for them—they are looking for you too)

a practice for heartbreak

feed yourself
spend three hours, four. care for yourself so slowly. treat yourself like your best friend. treat yourself like your own child. remind yourself that you are worth nourishing. remind yourself how your own hands can feed you. take time to connect to what is real—where your feet are, who is with you, who is not. notice where you numb. get sober from the vices that pull you out of the pain. your breaking heart is beautiful. be brave enough to stay.

let yourself drown
heartbreak is a tide. it will pull you under if you are not careful. i am asking you to not be careful. you will exhaust yourself more by fighting. there is a deep well of beauty waiting in your broken heart. there is an aliveness you can only feel when you are trembling under the weight of your own vulnerability. there is aliveness you can only feel from allowing yourself to break. notice how your edges have softened. feel the power in this state. go with it. remember that you, too, are this force. remember that this energy is your life. that this energy is not for trying to close the gap between you and another being. that this energy is for your creativity and connection to something bigger. your energy is begging to be poured into your actualization. another person was never meant to contain all of you—your own life was. so let yourself drown. gather up the water that surrounds you. pour it back into yourself. notice how the sky no longer falls for them. there is an aliveness that you can only feel when you step forward bravely because a part of you says softly—"try."

a practice for when you are ready to move on

have a funeral for the version of yourself you cannot carry with you
release the relics. release the ghosts. write a letter of who you were, who you have outgrown. thank this part of you. thank your past mistakes, for how they protected you. thank your past ways of being, for how they helped you survive. see how you did the best you could, with what you knew. write this letter with love. when you are ready—go outside. go near water. set the letter on fire. let this part of you go up in smoke as the page does.

imagine something new
even if you cannot see it yet. welcome this portal. everything must dissolve in order to become something new. trust the process of your becoming.

blythe

go where your heart feels like it can be the loudest

the unbearable beauty

there is nothing wrong with you
only rooms you drifted into
that were too small for you

a practice for anger

rage with it
rage with all that is wild within you and see that it is sacred. do not be afraid. find the part of you that knows your anger is honorable. find the invitation to what your soul knows to be true. be angry for the times your body was seen as someone else's territory. be angry for the ways you have been spiritually starved. be angry for what you have lost. be angry for the ways you can never go back. be angry for how you were allowed to leave yourself, again and again.

welcome it home
be a soft landing, an open door, for all the parts you have left behind. don't abandon yourself. not now. you've come too far for this.

a practice for belonging

leave where you call home
discover who you are in a new place. travel where you don't speak the language. discover what it's like to connect without needing to translate your soul. discover who you are outside of everything you've known.

tell a new story
tell the story that you matter here. that you belong here. that there is nothing left for you to do, fix, or reach for. that you do not owe us your suffering to reach your joy. that just by breathing, you have done enough. that you are protected here. that you are safe. that you deserve to be known.

a practice for becoming yourself

find a uniform
find what feels like you and wear it, over and over. notice what space this creates.

when you find yourself reaching too much—step back from the internet
the damage is never caused by the thing you are reaching towards, it is the reaching itself. wanting comes from coming in contact with a space inside of you. reaching is what happens when we mistake the space as something to fix. we reach toward other people's ideas of success, beauty, aliveness. this is so endlessly exasperated by the internet. there is so much to consume, to move towards. it is so easy to want someone else's life. and yet it is all smoke and mirrors when we step back. cleansing from this energy is an act of resistance to all that wants us to not pay attention. step away for a little longer than you think you can handle. let it be a tonic. record what you find.

ask more than you answer
when we are constantly trying to cling to certainty—our minds shut off in a way that we fail to realize. the big truth is

that we exist suspended in a grand unknown. i believe that this is the most uncomfortable thing for our human selves to hold, and, in a way, our desire to get out of this holding is the root of all suffering. the less we provide answers and the more we allow ourselves to humbly ask, staying open to uncertainty, the more we can clear our minds. see if you can feel in your body the difference between saying out loud, "i know this," versus, "why." feel that there is more to find.

stay on your path
we can spend our lives chasing something that shuts down our hearts because we are stuck on someone else's path out of fear of our own. you love what you love for a reason. our truest desires feel warm. there is no anxious grabbing or a fear-based chase. it's not something you can easily make sense of. these things that may feel insignificant are keys to your greatest gifts. open your mind to this possibility. give yourself this simplicity to allow what you love. take your life back. you're here for this.

blythe

so often, when we miss someone it is not them
but the version of ourselves we left behind
those are the parts of you that are waiting
on the doorstep of your awareness
reach out your hand
leave the light on
call yourself back home

the unbearable beauty

without the stories of us
without the stories of who i have been
without the stories that kept me alive
without the stories that kept me from the living
i found my center

how to open your creative channel

pay attention
being alive is an endlessly creative act. just by being here, you have the capacity to create. all that life asks of you is that you pay attention. notice the small things of beauty. notice the way dappled sunlight falls. the way a flower climbs out of the sidewalk, prevailing. the way an abandoned glove sits like an art piece against the white snow. pay attention to the sounds most people miss, the smell of your favorite places, the care in something attended to. now turn this attention inside.

open your heart
if you are wanting to create, there is something in you that is wanting to be known. in this life, you can protect your heart from this world, or you can be known. you will be asked again and again to open your heart. choose to be brave. choose to allow love to lead. to let go of the need to move through life hardened. to let go of the lie that this is a form of protection from all that has come before and all that the future holds. notice the space that opens inside of you when you soften your guard. now let life do what it does and rush through you. let me remind you—you are alive for this.

repeat, more honestly this time

how to make art (or something else important)

let it be mediocre
you do not have to be great. you do not have to be good. rather than using this as a permission slip to not give everything, use it as freedom to know that what you create deserves to stand on its own. if for nothing other than the fact that your heart is in it.

try not to hide
when you have done everything there is to do, and it is time to share—allow yourself to be revealed. be brave with it. do not hold yourself back from us. we need you.

every moment is a portal
every moment is a mirror

i have learned to regret nothing. there are opportunities that i have missed and versions of myself that i had to surrender to be who i am. there are people i needed to let go of, and i have had to break my own heart more times than i have wanted. but i am beginning to see how it all comes back to find you. how ten years from now, you can be living in the echo of an old dream. that you can never miss the life that is around you because your future is stretched out in front of you like the branches of an ancient banyan tree. how you can twist and turn as many times as you want. that nothing is ever truly missed. that nothing is ever truly lost.

living is an infinity mirror
it will all connect in the end
hatred
division
love
it is up to you to choose

living is an infinity mirror
you can keep reaching outwards
or you can open your eyes
open your mouth
and see what yells back

i am pouring into myself
i am a lone wolf, howling
i am wild
i am awake
i am alive
can you hear me?

i wish i could see me how you saw me back then, in my endless pursuit of falling apart. how in that i was still an obvious choice. how now we are looking at different people in that same way. how it was never really you. and it was never really me you were looking into, either. but what a gift it was, to come closer than arm's length. what a gift it is to still feel you here with me when the world goes quiet. i am imagining a more beautiful world that i don't have to tear apart. i'll wait for you there.

i want to see the wild landscapes of your life
the wild skies with all of their clouds over wild places
where your breath catches and where it flows freely
where you go when you are alone
who you are in the dark

what we must keep in order to live

keep a notebook. keep a record. keep a reminder. take note of the things that seem to hardly matter. take note of the things you swear you won't forget. because you most likely will, and i want you to remember. i want you to remember the small moments that felt like hope. i want you to remember the small cracks that became doorways. i want you to remember when life asked you to keep going. i want you to remember how you answered the question. i want you to remember the words they said that felt like a beginning. i want you to remember the very moment everything changed. i want you to remember the deep wells life threw you into without warning. i want you to remember so that when the cycle repeats itself, you know that you can survive.

keep a ritual. keep a practice. keep something sacred. keep a way of connecting to the force that runs through you. keep a way of finding this in the mundane. remember that most of your life is here. don't miss it. don't let your life pass you by as you wait for one moment. let the same walk you take every day be a re-reading. do it today. notice what you have missed before. find a new language. let each step be something entirely new. find refuge in your rituals. make your coffee in the name of beauty. make your art in the name of mediocrity. let this be enough. let your life be enough.

keep a vice. keep your soul as your compass, but keep yourself closer. stop trying to be perfect. stop trying to crawl your way out of the lessons of the living. stop trying to find a horizon in the void. stop waiting to wake up one day and be done. forgive yourself for trying. remember that you are inherently good. remember that you contain more than one thing. make the right choice. make the wrong choice. make the good bad right wrong choice. find yourself in something cosmic. find yourself in your five senses. light a candle. light a cigarette. let go a little. let yourself feel a little. stop acting like you're getting out alive. allow yourself to enjoy the ride.

keep an open heart. keep daring to soften. keep close to the ones who never need a translation of your soul. keep opening to the ones who speak an entirely different language. admit that you don't know everything just yet. accept that you never will. build a bridge between yourself and others with the desire to understand. build a bridge between everything you are and everything you wish to be with the hope that in this moment, just being here is enough. give that grace to others. see what happens. see how we are all a part of this story. stand up to injustice, and stay open to miracles. you're not in control, so stay open to magic. stay open to the fact that love has prevailed for centuries for you and i to be here. stay open to how life has chosen you, yet again. stay open to the things inside of you that whisper—*we're alive.*

all i want to hear is whatever soft thing
whispers inside of you
you're alive
you're alive
you're alive

the unbearable beauty

everything is hurting, and then life sends you an offering
everything is healing, and then life sends you a gift
you can't hold it together, and then life sends you a gift
you can't contain yourself, and then life sends you a gift
you've lost everything, and then life sends you a gift
you're scared to lose anything, and then life sends you a gift
life is beautiful and then it is a gift
life is unbearable and then it is an offering

i hope you feel it—
the unbearable beauty of being alive

thank you

to the ones who know my soul
and to the invisible forces that beg my heart to stay open

i keep going for you.

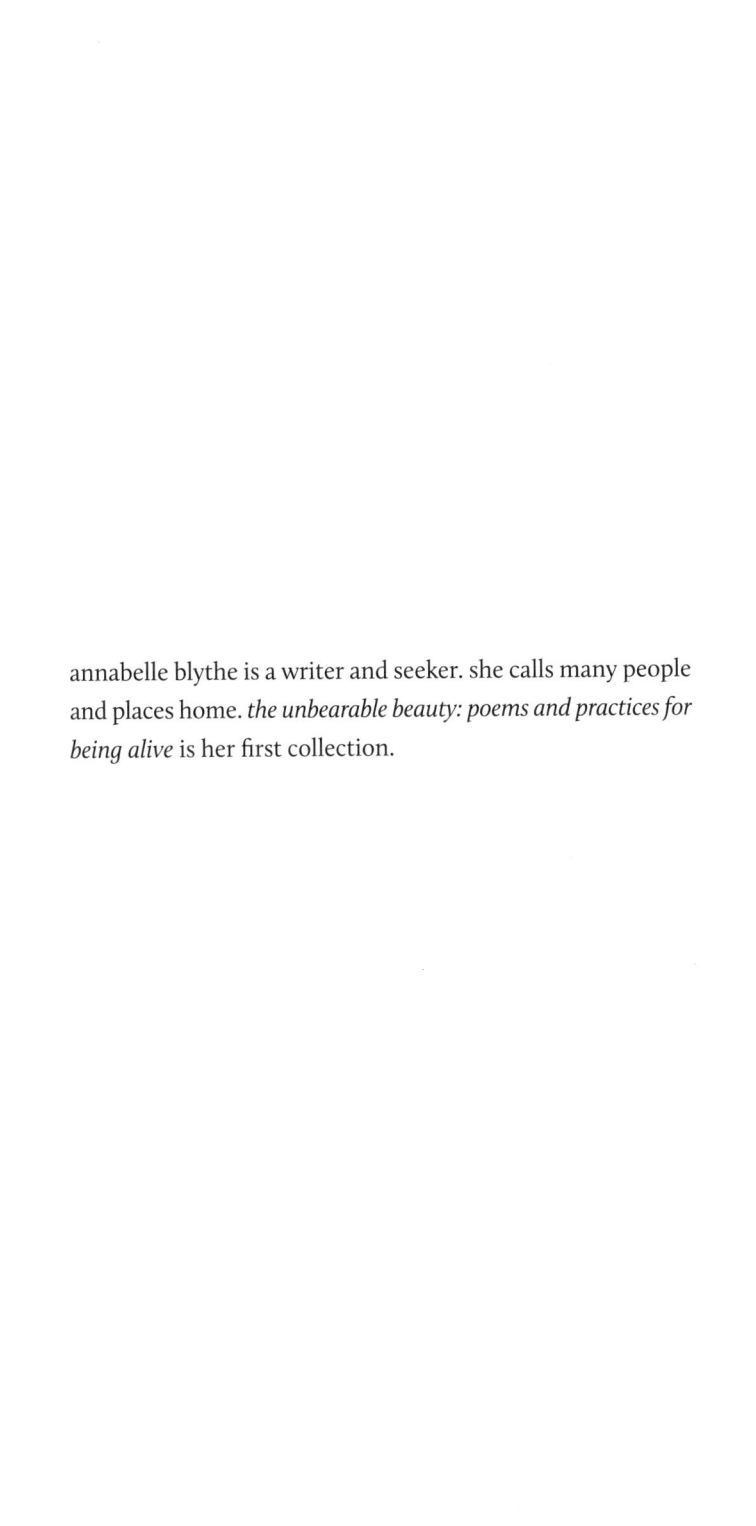

annabelle blythe is a writer and seeker. she calls many people and places home. *the unbearable beauty: poems and practices for being alive* is her first collection.

THOUGHT
CATALOG
Books

Thought Catalog Books is a publishing imprint of Thought Catalog, a digital magazine for thoughtful storytelling, and is owned and operated by The Thought & Expression Co. Inc., an independent media group based in the United States of America. Founded in 2010, we are committed to helping people become better communicators and listeners to engender a more exciting, attentive, and imaginative world. The Thought Catalog Books imprint connects Thought Catalog's digital-native roots with our love of traditional book publishing. The books we publish are designed as beloved art pieces. We publish work we love. Pioneering an author-first and holistic approach to book publishing, Thought Catalog Books has created numerous best-selling print books, audiobooks, and eBooks that are being translated in over 30 languages.

ThoughtCatalog.com | **Thoughtful Storytelling**

ShopCatalog.com | **Shop Books + Curated Products**

**MORE FROM
THOUGHT CATALOG BOOKS**

A Gentle Reminder
—*Bianca Sparacino*

When You're Ready, This Is How You Heal
—*Brianna Wiest*

This Was Meant To Find You
(When You Needed It Most)
—*Charlotte Freeman*

Holding Space for the Sun
—*Jamal Cadoura*

All That You Deserve
—*Jacqueline Whitney*

How Does It Feel?
—*Andrew Kearns*

THOUGHT
CATALOG
Books

THOUGHTCATALOG.COM